The
Revision Process

A guide for those months or years
between your first draft and your last

*To Julia — I'm honored to be part
of your journey. Hope this book
helps your write!*

by
Robin Stratton

Robin Stratton

With two bonus sections
by Rebecca Leo

The Revision Process

Heartfelt thanks to Lucy, Mom, Smitty, Rebecca, Tom, and Lee.

ISBN: 0-9753211-0-2

Printed in the United States of America

10 9 8 7 6 5 4 3 2 1

First Printing

Big Table Publishing Company
Newton, MA

www.BigTablePublishing.com

The difference between the right word and the almost right word is the difference between lightning and the lightning bug.

~ Mark Twain

TABLE OF CONTENTS

Introduction

Finally, your book is done! Or is it?

You've gone over your manuscript again and again. A year or five have passed since you began, and frankly, you're tired of looking at it. You have a synopsis and an outline, and a cover letter addressed to agents and publishers who claim to be looking for the type of book you've written. It's pretty much ready to go. But wait...

Is it really ready?

Every 6.2 seconds someone in the United States decides to write a book. Okay, I made that up. But the point is, a lot of people think writing a book is easy. They think all they have to do is come up with a good idea, write it down, send it out, and decide what to wear at the Academy Awards, because their book was made into a movie too, and only a few months after it won a Pulitzer.

But every book that has earned a spot on a shelf in a store has gone through a vigorous revision process that your book hasn't. Unless you're willing to subject your manuscript to the same harshly-critical evaluation, you won't be able to compete.

Take a look at your book

Are you dissatisfied with any part of it? Is there a chapter you're not crazy about, or a character who isn't well defined? Does your story get off to a slow start? Does the plot falter in some places? Does the ending feel contrived? Are some scenes boring, even to you?

Not sure? Pay attention to your reaction the next time a friend asks to read your book. Are you excited about showing it, or reluctant?

If you don't feel comfortable letting a friend read your book, why would you consider it ready to submit to an agent or a publisher?

Maybe it's not ready

Your novel is like your child. You only want to hear good things about it. You know that if you drop off a hungry, muddy, whining brat with a friend, you're not going to return in a few hours to rave reviews.

Like your child, your book has to be cleaned up and lovingly disciplined to correct the bad habits that can be annoying to others and a source of embarrassment to you.

"The End" is just the beginning

When an artist finishes a painting, it's done. When a ball player hits the winning home run in the bottom of the ninth, the game is over and the Red Sox have lost again. But when you type those magic words "The End," all it means is that you've made it to the end of the first draft. You're only half done! Now it's time to refine your book. That means tightening, trimming, fleshing out scenes, and re-examining every word.

But I can't do it again!

How do you go over your book again when you're so sick of it you could scream?

You just do it. You have to. Writing a book is really hard. That's why most people don't do it. But you're not "most people." You said you were going to write a book, and you did it. You wrote a book!

And now you're going to write it again.

But this time you're not alone. This time you have a guide to help you through the revision process.

How this book is different

There are hundreds of books on the market about writing. Books I used to buy until I noticed an unnerving trend: most books about writing are written by writers who have only written books about writing! And while they provide decent, easy-to-follow suggestions for getting started, and then tell you what to do when it's time to approach an agent, they don't offer any direction for all those months or years between the first draft and the final draft.

This is not a book about writing. This is a book about writing better. Better than you thought you could. Pushing yourself to rewrite and refine the same chapters over and over until every single sentence performs.

What this book promises

As you learn to recognize and fix problems, you will not only produce a better book, you will become a better writer.

Rewriting is Refining
The revision process takes more time than writing the book.

After you finish your book, you send out proposals. Right? Wrong. Too many writers submit too soon.

The spell of "It's done!" and the sad aftermath

Basking in the glow of having reached the end of their book, most writers begin the search for an agent. They consider their book "as ready as it'll ever be," and with innocent trust, send out query letters, then wait for the phone to ring. Some indulge in fantasies about a bidding war. Only takes two publishers to want you, and you're looking at millions of dollars!

But agents are canny and unreasonable. They have this habit of rejecting manuscripts that are badly written. Something to do with not wanting to lose money or ruin their credibility. It's weird.

So what arrives in the mail is not an invitation to send your entire manuscript and anything else you've ever written. No. You're thanked, turned down, and wished the best of luck placing your work elsewhere. Oh, and please forgive the form letter.

What should you do?

Feel rage. Be stunned and indignant. Not one of those agents understood your vision! How did they get to be agents if they can't understand a person's vision?

Accept the pity of others. Put the manuscript in a box and put the box in the closet. You'll look at it in a year or two. Maybe by then you can find an agent who appreciates quality literature.

Or you can ask yourself, *Are all those rejection slips in any way related to my writing?* Maybe "as ready as it'll ever be" isn't good enough.

Step One: Admit you have a problem

Most of my clients bring in their manuscript hoping that I'll return it with wide-eyed, startled-into-silence approval. They've come to me for help, but deep down, they don't want criticism. They want me to say, *Your first draft is perfect! Don't change a thing!*

How do I know? Because every time I show my manuscript to someone, that's what I want to hear. In my fantasy, they even laugh. *Get outta here,* they say. *This book is ready to go right now!*

But the fact is, early drafts are never perfect. Much the same way that you're not going to lose ten pounds overnight by taking a pill, you're not going to create the book you dreamed of without a lot of hard work. Remember all those hours you spent writing? Multiply that number by at least three. That's revision time.

The road to recovery

The grueling revision process involves giving up bad habits; recognizing what you've been doing wrong, and training yourself to do it right.

There will be long, sleepless nights. Tremors. Eating binges. Too much soda, coffee, sugar. Sweaty palms and racing heart. At times you'll wonder if you're going to make it through.

One word at a time

There is only one way to perfect your book, and that's word by word. Slowly. With every brutal intention of making changes. You're not looking for good stuff now; this isn't about patting yourself on the back. Don't cut corners and don't coast over the parts you think are "probably okay." This time you mean business.

Aloud is allowed

Read everything out loud. Every. Single. Word. Listen carefully. Is the dialogue authentic, or have you used words that no one ever actually says, like "recalcitrant?" Do you tend to overuse some words? Do you vary sentence structure, or do they all sound the same?

Please don't be one of those writers who thinks they don't need to do this!

Why Did You Write the Book?

Are you writing for yourself and your family, or is your goal to be published?

Whether you've written a novel, your memoirs, or a book about World War II, it's important to clarify your intention. Why you write influences how you write. If you're planning to win the attention of an agent or publisher, you need to learn the literary techniques that engage readers with dynamic characters, action-packed drama, rising tension, a powerful climax, and a satisfying resolution.

Real life

A woman marries a man then discovers he's abusive. She gets pregnant four times, and each time he accuses her of having been unfaithful and beats her. He beats the kids, too. After ten years, she finally escapes.

Another decade passes, and the woman feels it's time to share her story of survival. She hopes it will help other women trapped in an abusive marriage.

Real monotony

She writes the story of her life in novel form, describing how she met her husband, and how he lured her in with his attractive, charismatic personality, and his earnest promise to make her happy. She writes about the first time he hit her, then the second time, then the third, then the twentieth. As children join the story, there are more beating scenes with screaming and crying and numerous vows to escape. Chapter after chapter blend together in a marathon of torture. The result is *not* mounting tension; on the contrary, each scene is so much like the one before it that emotional impact dwindles. Before long readers feel impatient or bored. They might begin to skim, or worse, put the book down and not return to it.

What I would do

If the author of this book came to me, I would ask her why she's writing her story. Is it for herself and her children? Or is she hoping to sell it so that it gets into the hands of the women who need it?

If she wants to stay faithful to the facts, that's fine. But she might have trouble getting an agent interested.

If she wants her story to sell, she needs to revise it in order to enhance drama.

This is difficult for some writers. Straying from "what really happened" feels a little bit like lying. But it's not. Honest.

Ask yourself, *Am I interested in documenting the events as they really happened at the risk of readership, or do I want to tell the story in a way that's most compelling?*

Enhancing drama

Four kids means four pregnancy scenes, four birth scenes, coming up with four names, and achieving four distinct personalities. For the sake of a novel, two children works better, and focus stays on the action, not on learning names and personalities.

Too many descriptions of beatings will dilute drama. Instead of repeating scenes, spend time exploring how this character wound up in an abusive relationship. What was her childhood like? Was she abused as a kid, too? Is there a pattern?

Each time she decides she's not going to take it anymore, she leads readers into thinking *Finally, this is it!* When she doesn't leave, they feel tricked or annoyed. Sympathy fades. By the time she does escape, the drama of the scene has been skinned to the bone. Readers don't get to applaud her courage because they put the book down two chapters ago.

"But... but... but..."

By this time my client has slumped in her seat. She thought the manuscript was pretty much ready to go; she's been over it half a dozen times and even her daughter likes it. Now she has to totally redo the whole thing? She says she can't. I tell her she can. She says she can't! I tell her she can. She says she hates me.

Revised!

Next time she comes in all excited. Her story, no longer a boring litany of abuse, is powerful with drama, pace and substance. As soon as she began writing about her main character's childhood she discovered all kinds of self-destructive behaviors that she never realized were part of the pattern. She's so glad she took my advice. She doesn't hate me anymore.

Now her book has a chance of being published. Trimming repetitious details that drag down action has made her story exciting.

This applies to non-fiction too

No one would advise tampering with the facts if you're reporting a non-fiction account of an adventure, an award, or a remarkable survival, achievement, or discovery. But clarifying why you wrote the book helps you determine the best way to reach your target audience.

Curing Cancer by Michael Waldholtz could have been a dense, scientific textbook about the history of the discovery of DNA and the subsequent search for the gene associated with breast cancer. Waldholtz, a knowledgeable, gifted writer, would have established himself as a respectable medical reporter, but he would have limited his audience to academics. In order to make his book accessible to as many people as possible, he made the story exciting even to readers without a scientific or medical background. He presented the information using plenty of dialogue, vivid descriptions, and easy-to-understand language. The result is a dynamic, briskly-paced account of fierce competition, heartbreak, and triumph, with characters who are dedicated, crafty, sneaky, and human.

Your options

Writing your memoirs for yourself or your family means sticking to the facts without enhancing drama. Optimize reader interest by telling your story with well-crafted dialogue and action.

Writing because you have a remarkable story means the drama is built in, so you don't have to change much. Sharpen your skills by learning the literary techniques that keep you focused on the all-important elements of plot, character development, climax and resolution.

Writing to get published doesn't mean you have to turn your back on integrity and write according to a formula. But if you want your book to sell, you need to engage readers right away, keep them involved, create suspense, and make a lasting impact.

Ask yourself, *Am I writing for myself, or am I trying to get published?* Be honest!

Subj: The Revision Process
Date: 2/13/2004 12:01:03 PM Eastern Standard Time
From: cmstratton@attbi.com
To: BigTableCo@aol.com

I started a list of things I don't like when I read a novel. Maybe you can use them, maybe not. No offense taken :-)

Descriptions of a woman's wardrobe in scene after scene.

What characters ordered for breakfast, lunch, and dinner.

Type of wine they chose and why.

A female character who is a real success story, but so blatantly wise and obnoxious that it turns you off instead of on.

Mysteries that go out of their way to mislead you into thinking you know who-dunnit and then come up with something out of the blue that you weren't privy to, and therefore couldn't know in order to solve the mystery yourself.

Prologues that don't give you a clue as to the time of the Prologue versus the story itself.

Heroines who are always dieting!

Love, Mom

The Elements of Plot
Does your book have everything it needs?

When you're unclear about where your story is headed, your writing will lack direction and focus. Identify and optimize these key plot elements: setting and status quo; character goals, reactions and choices; storyline and theme; climax and resolution.

Setting and status quo

What happens when the status quo is disrupted? There's an unexpected turn of events, conditions change, and characters are forced to change too.

Picture a charming New England town with shady, tree-lined streets, a small family-run supermarket, and a grassy park where ragtime concerts are held each Thursday evening in the summer; the kind of place where everyone knows everyone else. The mayor, a handsome, shy, gentle-tempered bachelor in his mid-40s, walks out of his house one morning and finds a crack in his driveway that wasn't there the night before. As he walks to town he notices that the sidewalk is cracked, too. When he gets to the corner, he sees a long, deep crack running all the way down Maple Street. At that moment he feels the rumblings of a powerful earthquake.

Ask yourself, *What is the status quo as my story begins?*

Wreak extra havoc

Unleash chaos in the right setting and amplify the difference between before and after. A charming New England town usually has to deal with charming New England town problems, not earthquakes. Consider how the drama changes if the setting is New York City, a busy, ambulance-filled place accustomed to disaster; or the uninhabited plains of the midwest, where an earthquake might go undetected.

On a personal level, a torrid affair will impact a happy marriage differently than a marriage already on the brink of divorce. A diagnosis of breast cancer has different implications for a young fashion model than for a woman in her 80s who lives in a nursing home.

Ask yourself, *Does my setting promote maximum drama?*

How characters react and choose

Which scenario is more interesting?

A man known for his courage loses the use of his legs after he's nearly killed by a drunk driver. He bravely accepts his new condition and continues to lead a meaningful life.

Or:

The town's most drunken, vile bum loses the use of his legs in an accident he caused when he stumbled off the sidewalk into the path of an oncoming car. The driver, a young mother of twins, is killed trying to avoid hitting him. He battles depression, guilt, despair, and wishes he could just die. But when another disaster forces him to chose between life and death, he realizes how much he wants to live, and he decides to redeem himself by helping others.

Ask yourself, *How did my characters react when the status quo was disrupted? What choices did they make?*

What do your characters want?

When characters have a clear goal, usually one of two things happens:

They get what they want, but only after a long, hard struggle. The theme of never giving up will always be popular because it suggests that we live in a purposeful world where we can get what we want if we are willing to work hard and believe in ourselves.

Make readers care about what happens to your characters. Build suspense by showing there's a strong possibility that characters could fail; litter the path to success with plenty of obstacles.

They don't get what they want, but they get what they need. Sometimes characters risk everything to get what they think they want, only to discover that the ability to live without leads to something better - independence or freedom. The theme of gaining priceless insight appeals to readers who like to see characters find strength from within.

Validate your characters' new wisdom by giving them what they think they want, and letting them make the decision that they're better off without it.

Ask yourself, *What do my characters want?*

Tell us a couple of stories

Your primary plot should blend in a meaningful way with secondary plots.

When an earthquake hits a quiet New England town, a man paralyzed from the waist down, because of an accident he caused when he was drunk, gets trapped in the hospital after a section of it collapses. The mayor, who happens to be the uncle of a woman who was killed in the same accident, has to put aside his anger and help with the rescue. A beautiful young fashion model, buried beneath rubble, tells the paramedic she didn't survive a mastectomy and two months of chemotherapy to die on the corner of Maple and Elm. The paramedic, a happily married man, has no idea his wife is also trapped - in a hotel room where she's having a torrid affair with his closest buddy.

So, what's your book about?

The question writers dread. Most of us have lived with our book for years, but can't deliver a concise and comprehensive description of what it's about. We begin talking about characters and scenes, then get bogged down telling the message of the book and explaining how readers are supposed to feel at the end. We watch the spark of interest fade from the eyes of our listener, and conclude lamely, "It's sort of hard to explain..."

The trouble is, we're so close to our book that we can't differentiate between *what happens* in the book and what the book is *about*.

Storyline and theme

When people ask what your is book about, they want to know the storyline: In Kafka's *Metamorphosis*, a guy wakes up one morning to find himself transformed into a huge, disgusting insect. That's what happens. Genre fiction focuses on storyline:

Western	good vs. evil
Mystery	who did what and why
Romance	falling in love despite the odds
Horror	human vs. supernatural or erratic personality

Ask yourself, *What happens in my book?*

Mainstream and **literary fiction** have a second, deeper layer; a theme woven into the fabric of the plot. *The Metamorphosis* is also about a man confronting his terrifying sense of alienation.

After Cole Porter finished writing *Showboat*, he wanted one more song to tie the whole story together. "Old Man River" reassures us that no matter what happens in this life - who you're with, where you live, how you die - it's good to know that some things, like the mighty Mississippi, remain the same.

Gone With The Wind is a story about the Civil War. The theme is survival. *Anna Karenina* is about a married woman who has an affair, then commits suicide. The theme is despair. *To Kill a Mockingbird* is about the trial of a black man accused of raping a white woman in 1930s Alabama. The theme is racism.

Books with themes endure because readers relate to universal emotions, even if they've never fought in a war, had an affair, or sat in a court room.

Raise the quality of your book by working in a theme. Chances are, you've already planted the seed - friendship, betrayal, sinister technology - and by clarifying what it is, you will be able to flesh it out. You'll see your story and characters take on more depth.

Ask yourself, *What are some of the themes in my book?*

Climax

The first part of your book sets the stage for the point when something's got to give: a drunken bum who's lost the use of his legs in an accident he caused wants only to be left alone so he can die. But when an earthquake destroys the hospital and traps him inside, he's faced with a life changing decision: give up and die, or help those who are trapped with him.

Build up to a climax by clarifying what it will mean for your characters. The paralyzed bum's decision to be brave isn't just about saving lives; it's about taking responsibility, breaking patterns, and wanting to survive in a meaningful way. Never again will he doubt the beauty and the blessing that is life.

Ask yourself, *What is the climax of my book? What does it mean for the main characters?*

Resolution

Sometimes clients tell me they have no idea how their book is going to end; all they have is "this cool idea." That's okay. Keep writing, and an ending will emerge. What's important is getting the first draft done.

But when it comes to refining your book, you need to know from page one where you're going.

Many writers lose steam as they approach the end, and they hurry up and dispense fate. This character drops dead, those two get married, and these two split up. Relying on sudden and contrived circumstances no one knew about - a brain tumor, a secret romance, a husband who works for the CIA - is cheating. Readers deserve an ending that's surprising but logical and compelling, with hints dropped along the way. *Oh, that's what those pills in the medicine cabinet were for!* You can even mislead a reader - the husband who made those late night phone calls isn't having an affair after all; he works for the CIA - if you play fair and give clues.

Prepare for the ending from the beginning.

Ask yourself, *What has to get resolved in my book?*

Section Dissection

Like big cities, manuscripts have good sections
and bad sections.

The good sections

The good sections have been cleaned up and are fun to visit. Nothing gets past the Language Police who constantly prowl the streets in search of words that don't belong. Every resident is trim and effective.

The bad sections

Lurking in the bad sections are unrefined, unshaven sentences that have been allowed to stay despite their bad behavior. Heavy-handed descriptions hang around, resisting all efforts to rehabilitate. No one monitors the bad sections, and gangs of poor word choices flourish unchecked. These are the sections we hurry past, and try not to be in after dark.

I'm always surprised at how many writers are willing to turn their backs on the bad sections, or pretend they don't exist. Sometimes I'll point out a phrase I think is awkward or cliché, and my client will say, "Oh that's been there since the beginning." As if that makes it okay.

Other writers assume someone else will do the job. The editors at Doubleday, maybe. After all, they're the experts. They know how to "handle" the bad sections.

It's up to you

There's only one way to earn the approval of an agent, and that's by submitting a book that is *all* good section.

It's time to visit the sections you're not comfortable with. Time to hunt down the rogue words, clear them out, and replace them with words that are responsible and hard working.

Grab your red pen, we're going in.

Big Fat Rogue Words
How did they get there? Who let them in?

Sometimes words come in and take up residence. At first we think they're okay and don't question them. Then they let some of their friends in, and their friends let their friends in. And suddenly there's a vibe in the neighborhood that's not good, not good at all. There's too much noise, and cigarettes on front lawns, and broken-down cars parked in driveways. It's those rogue words we let in! They slow down, clutter up, and spoil the look of our carefully-manicured sentences.

Understanding why it's wrong

When I was in school I was bad in math, and I used to ask my brother to help me with my homework. I realize now what a good teacher he was, but back then, when he tried to explain the rules, I would get frustrated and say, "Don't tell me how to do it, just tell me the answer!"

New clients accept my feedback and make the changes I suggest without understanding *why* a sentence lacks impact or is cumbersome. They recognize that a revised sentence sounds better, but they can't say why. With practice, they learn to be on the lookout for mistakes, and can implement the techniques to fix them.

Like math, writing is right or wrong according to certain rules. All words, like all numbers, are good; but they have to be in the right place. Good writing reflects an understanding of the rules.

Neighborhood Watch

Be on the lookout for rogue words. If you come upon them, demand to know why they are there. Do they have a job to do, or are they just hanging around? If they can't offer a good reason for being in the sentence, get rid of them.

Rather, quite, somewhat

Some words are rather weak. They are quite distracting, somewhat annoying, and don't add anything.

Not only do these words serve no purpose, they make your writing sound imprecise. If I said I was "rather nervous" the first time I donated blood, would you have an understanding of how nervous I was? If I told you I was "somewhat excited" about eating pie tonight, could you form a picture in your mind of how excited I was?

Be clear and direct in order to evoke an image or an emotion.

Avoid repetition

Don't squander a reader's attention by saying the same thing twice.

> **Aaron looked at his watch. It was almost midnight. Time to go. He poked Tim with his foot and woke him up.**
> **"Wake up, Tim," he said. "It's almost midnight. We gotta go."**

Don't be dull, boring, or uninteresting

As a writer, you're supposed to paint a picture with your words. But beware of a tendency to use multiple descriptive words that mean the same thing.

> **He couldn't bear to look at her gloomy, glum expression for another day.**

Using both "gloomy" and "glum" is excessive. Cut one.

> **Her beautiful dress was made of lovely soft silk fabric that was a gorgeous deep, rich, dark red.**

Eliminate the repetitious words, and get to the point:

> **Her beautiful silk dress was garnet red.**

Very

There's no law against using the word "very:"

He walked very fast.
She was very happy to hear the news.
Her project was very good.

But "very" isn't as precise as a single stronger word:

He hurried.
She was delighted to hear the news.
Her project was excellent.

Don't combine "very" with words that are already powerful; for example, very terrified, very furious, very terrible, very adorable.

A phrase I hear often is "very unique." To call something "very unique" is just plain wrong. Since "unique" means one of a kind, something is unique or it isn't.

Don't utilize "utilize"

"Utilize" does *not* mean "use." It means to use something for a purpose other than that for which it was intended, as in "I utilized a spoon to dig my way out of prison." Utilize is a word people like because they think it sounds fancy. I call it a "resume word." Everyone looking for a better job wants to "utilize skills." But unless you're using those skills for a different purpose - "I want to utilize my acting skills to impress women" - you *use* skills.

When "badly" is bad

When you want something "badly" it doesn't mean you want it a lot; it means your ability to want is impaired, the same way that "I drive badly" means you don't drive well. If you say "I want to play tennis so badly!" it doesn't mean you're really in the mood to play tennis; it means that you want to play tennis with a lack of skill. If you had a baby and someone asked, "How do you feel?" you wouldn't say, "I feel gladly!"

Kick out extra words

	Before	**After**
	He answered the phone that was in the kitchen.	He answered the kitchen phone.
	She was happier than she had ever been before.	She was happier than she had ever been.
	After the surgery he was never the same again.	After the surgery he was never the same.
	He could feel the beads of sweat that were forming on his forehead.	He could feel beads of sweat forming on his forehead.
	They met at the meeting that they were both at.	They met at the meeting.
	She worked all morning long.	She worked all morning.
	Every time he sang, people were always surprised.	Every time he sang, people were surprised.
	He whispered quietly in my ear.	He whispered in my ear.
	I'll do it, I thought to myself.	*I'll do it*, I thought.
	I gave you my number but you still haven't called me yet.	I gave you my number but you still haven't called me.

"Seem" often seems like a waste of time

"Seem" is one of those words that sometimes sneaks in where it's not welcome, and makes all the words around it feel weak, because it implies uncertainty.

My answer seemed to delight him and he threw back his head and laughed.

If he threw his head back and laughed, my answer *did* delight him. See how much stronger the sentence is without it:

My answer delighted him and he threw back his head and laughed.

"Seem" undermines the integrity of a descriptive word:

Mildred seemed horrified that her son had a pet rat.

Ditch "seem" and optimize power:

Mildred was horrified that her son had a pet rat.

My rule is: whenever you see the word "seem," try reading the sentence without it and see how it sounds.

Write "really" well

I'm really sure you're really tired of me telling you about all the words that really sound really bad when you really don't use them the right way.

People think "really" adds power to the word after it. And sometimes it does. But like "very," too often "really" is used with a word that only occurs in one degree.

For example, the word "sure" in the paragraph above. Technically, there's no such thing as being *really sure*. Sure is sure. If you're not sure, you're unsure.

However, there are plenty of degrees of tired. You can be tired, and you can be *really tired.*

Another reason "really" gets overused is because it has two meanings. It can boost the volume of an adjective: *She was really mad;* or it can mean "truly," as in, *I really think you need help.*

Before using "really," decide what function you want it to perform. And just for kicks, see how the sentence sounds without it.

Take the time to be brief

My mom worked as a secretary an undisclosed number of years ago for a boss who was a master at dictating letters that were concise - short and straight to the point. On one particularly busy day he dictated a letter that was longer than normal, and concluded with an apology: "Sorry for the long letter - I didn't have time to write a short one." Like Mark Twain (who said this first, unless my mom is older than she says) her boss knew it took extra time, effort, and skill to weed out all the unnecessary words.

Right It

Get rid of extra words that clutter up and slow down

Achieving Authentic Dialogue
Conversations between characters should say a lot.

Dialogue isn't just talking; it's the best way to develop the plot, define characters, and let readers in on a secret.

Develop the plot

Every writer faces the temptation to report events, rather than involve readers in a scene:

> **Matilda discovered she was pregnant, and she knew the news would make her husband Hank angry, so she went to the bank, took out all the money, and hid it in a can in the garage for when she decided to leave him.**

But blocks and blocks of unbroken text is a turn off. Many readers will reject a book that looks like it doesn't have enough dialogue. Let a scene play itself out:

> **Matilda's hand was trembling so hard that she could barely dial her sister's number.**
>
> **"Pick up, pick up," she muttered. "Hello?"**
>
> **"Matilda?"**
>
> **"Yeah. Hi."**
>
> **"What did the doctor say?"**
>
> **"I'm three months pregnant."**
>
> **"Oh God. Matilda, what are you going to do? Are you going to tell Hank?"**
>
> **"I can't. He'll freak."**
>
> **"So what will you do?"**
>
> **Matilda touched her abdomen. Was she showing yet? "I'm going to leave him."**
>
> **"Thank God. When?"**
>
> **"As soon as I can. I'm on my way to the bank right now. I'm going to empty the account. Take all the money and hide it. And when he goes to work tomorrow, I'll pack and leave."**

Involve readers by giving them the opportunity to experience a scene firsthand.

Define characters

Dialogue has to reflect the voice of your main characters; their vocabulary, the way they express themselves, their strengths and weaknesses as communicators. Craft dialogue to show, not tell:

When Matilda came home with the money, she was annoyed to see Hank awake and watching television. He was so disgusting. She hated the way he always swore and criticized her. Never once did he have something nice to say! He never thanked her for everything she did around the house, for all the meals she cooked, all the laundry she did. And the way he talked sounded so ignorant.

Telling readers what to think of Hank - that he's disgusting, mean, and ignorant - cheats them out of the opportunity to find out on their own, and impact is diminished. Here's how to *show* what Hank is like:

Matilda came back from the bank with over two thousand dollars in her purse. She was hoping Hank would still be asleep, but no, there he was in his usual spot on the sofa, parked in front of the television, drinking a beer.

"This here's a good show." He pointed with the hand that held the can. "Answer questions and win a buncha money. I should be on this show. I'm smarter than that guy, and he just won three hundred bucks!"

"I'll be right back," Matilda said. "I left something in the car."

She started to go, but he called her back, barked out her name: "Tildy, get me another brew! If you can find it in that refrigerator. It's a mess in there! You gotta get rid of some of those leftovers!"

Readers get to see Hank in action, instead of just being told by the writer what he's like.

Let readers in on a secret

Sometimes you want readers to know something before a character knows it. Here's how to do it in a way that's boring:

When Hank said that he was going to the bank to get some money to pay the snow removal guy, Matilda didn't want him to know that she'd emptied the account, so she told him she would go instead.

Involve readers by letting the scene play itself out with dialogue:

"I'm going to the bank," Hank said.

Matilda was cleaning out the refrigerator, but stopped to face him. "What? Why?"

"Need to pay the snow removal guy. He don't take MasterCard. Ha ha!"

"Can't you write him a check?"

"Nah, he wants cash."

"How much? Let me get my purse, maybe I have it."

"You don't got fifty bucks," Hank said. "Gimme the car keys."

Matilda closed the refrigerator door. "Why don't I go? I don't mind. I need a break. You stay here and watch your show."

Eliminate
unrealistic dialogue

Dialogue that sounds unnatural can steal a scene, and *not* in a good way.

> "I'm going to the supermarket," Matilda said. "Plus I've quite a few other errands to run as well."
> Hank didn't even look up from the TV. "That will be just fine."
> "I will be gone for a long time. I have a lot of things I need to buy. For instance, we need kitty litter for Cissie, our cat."
> "Okay. So long, Matilda."
> "So long, Hank. I will see you when I come back home."

Try:

> "I'm going to the supermarket, Hank," Matilda said.
> He didn't even look up from the TV. "Okay."
> "I might be a while. I'll see you later."
> "Bye."

But don't be
too realistic!

Empty words and phrases that pepper natural conversation can slow down the action in your writing.

> She was almost out the door when Hank called her back.
> "Tildy?"
> "What," she said. "What do you want?"
> "Guess what?"
> "What?"
> "We're outta ice cream."
> "Oh."
> "So, can you get some?"
> "Okay."
> "Okay."

Trim, stay focused, and keep action moving:

> **She was almost out the door when Hank called her back.**
> **"We're out of ice cream," he said. "Can you get some?"**
> **"Okay."**
> **"Bye."**

Pay attention!

One of the most common mistakes writers make is having one character pose a question, and then forgetting to have the other character answer:

> **"Did you see your mother yet?" Hank asked.** **Matilda's mother hadn't recovered fully from the stroke.** *She might never be the same after this,* **Hank thought.** *Might not be able to keep her dogs, even.* **Something he knew would kill her - her dogs were her life.**
> **"I gotta call my sister," Matilda said. "I'll see you later."**

Just as bad is a response that isn't logical or authentic:

> **"Did you go see your mother yet?" Hank asked.** **Matilda's mother hadn't recovered fully from the stroke.** *She might never be the same after this,* **Hank thought.** *Might not be able to keep her dogs, even.* **Something he knew would kill her - her dogs were her life.**
> **"I haven't seen her yet," Matilda said.**

A more realistic response would be "No."

Say something worthwhile

Make sure that every exchange of dialogue serves a purpose.

> **Matilda walked into the bank and saw her favorite clerk. She went up to his window and handed him her withdrawal slip.**

"Hi, Johnny," she said.

"Hi, Matilda," he said. "What are you up to today?"

"Not too much. Took the car out to get it washed."

"I should do that too."

"You really should," Matilda said. "Too much rust builds up and you can get real problems."

"Yeah, that's what my dad always says. That I should take better care of my car."

"He's right. Who's got money to buy a new car these days?"

"Not me."

"Me either."

Ask yourself, *Do all the conversations between my characters serve a purpose?*

When your book is made into a movie...

The director is not going to suggest you appear on screen to explain that someone is selfish or jealous or secretly in love with someone else's husband. He's going to want that stuff to be shown.

The same holds true for your book. Telling readers what they're supposed to think is just plain lazy.

Instead of telling:

Matilda felt like her mother never approved of anything she did, even though she said she loved her.

Use dialogue to show:

Matilda's mother's spoke in a weary tone that suggested she had suffered more than her share, "Far be it from me to make judgements

about the crazy things you do. **Even though I don't understand why you act this way, or why you say those terrible things to me, I still love you."**

Won't it be boring if I write out every scene?

Yes, very. The following scene doesn't affect the story so it's okay to just report:

> **Matilda wanted to make her mother a birthday cake, but she was out of vanilla. She checked her watch - just enough time to go to the store. She told Hank she'd be back in a few minutes, and when she returned, he was still watching TV.**

But write out scenes when something significant happens:

> **Matilda wanted to make her mother a birthday cake, but when she looked in the cabinet she saw she was out of vanilla. She checked her watch - just enough time to go to the store. She told Hank she'd be back in a few minutes.**
> **"Whatever," he said.**
> **It irritated her that he didn't get up from the couch to kiss her; he didn't even look at her. *Stupid TV. One of these days I should just put it out with the trash.* For the millionth time, she thought about what it would be like to leave him.**
> **She decided to go to the market up the street. Less selection and more expensive than the grocery store on Elm, but she didn't have any extra time; she was cutting it close as it was.**

"Oh my God, I don't believe it... Matty?"

Only one person called her that. Dismayed, she turned around, and there was Brian. Their one-night stand six years ago had left her pregnant. The decision to have an abortion was something she'd regretted ever since, and even now her mother liked to throw it in her face like scalding water - *Wonder what that little child would be like, if you'd had him?*

"Wow. Brian. Hi."

Ask yourself, *Does this scene impact the story? Or is it just time passing while characters go about their day?*

Right It

Maintain a sense of immediacy by letting readers experience scenes through dialogue.

Attributes for Amateurs

"Please read this section," she begged
and implored beseechingly.

When characters snarl, gasp, whimper, shout, sob, and retort, readers begin to get numb. Overuse of colorful attributes takes away from their individual impact. And when you explain how dialogue is delivered, you cheat readers out of the chance to interpret the language on their own.

Written or overwritten?

There's nothing wrong with a punchy attribute here and there. A word like "scold" paints an immediate picture. But writers who go out of their way to make every attribute spectacular usually wind up sounding amateurish, especially when the attribute is followed by an action-packed adverb.

> **"I don't want you near him!" Jan shouted hysterically.**
> **"I don't care!" Elaine screamed angrily. "Ed and I are going out tonight and there's nothing you can do about it!"**

"Said" says it best

Most of your attributes should be "said." "Said" is well-behaved and gets along with every other word. Not interested in competing or showing off, "said" lets well-crafted dialogue portray emotions without relying on attributes that sound contrived or overdone.

The other team player is "told." Like "said," "told" stays in the background and lets language do its job.

> **"I don't want you near him," Jan said. She even raised her fist, a dramatic gesture that Elaine found ridiculous.**
> **"I don't care," Elaine told her. "Ed and I are going out tonight, and there's nothing you can do about it."**

35

Don't use multiple attributes

A paragraph rarely features more than one speaker, so using more than one attribute isn't necessary:

> "I don't want you near him," Jan said. She even raised her fist, a dramatic gesture that Elaine found ridiculous.
> "I don't care," Elaine told her. "Ed and I are going out tonight, and there's nothing you can do about it," she continued.

Sometimes nothing is better

Vary sentence structure by crafting dialogue that doesn't require an attribute:

> "I don't want you near him," Jan said. She even raised her fist, a dramatic gesture that Elaine found ridiculous.
> "I don't care," Elaine told her. "Ed and I are going out tonight, and there's nothing you can do about it."
> Jan smiled menacingly. "I wouldn't be so sure."
> "What do you mean?"
> "I think you know."

On the other hand...

Line after line of unassigned dialogue can get confusing.

> "I don't want you near him," Jan said. She even raised her fist, a dramatic gesture that Elaine found ridiculous.
> "I don't care," Elaine told her. "Ed and I are going out tonight, and there's nothing you can do about it."
> "I wouldn't be so sure."
> "What do you mean?"
> "I think you know."
> "Well I was with him last night, and he didn't even mention you."

"That's a lie! I was with him last night!"
"What time?"
"Just before 9:00."
"He showed up at my apartment, drunk, at midnight."

Having to go back up and figure out which woman said what takes readers out of the scene.

Ask yourself, *Am I going overboard with the attributes, or am I letting the dialogue speak for itself?*

Subj: The Revision Process
Date: 2/15/2004 2:23:10 PM Eastern Standard Time
From: cmstratton@attbi.com
To: BigTableCo@aol.com

I thought of a few more things I don't like. I spoke to Karen, and she came up with some, too.

When the author goes into way too much detail about a subject just to show they are knowledgeable about it

When too many individual scenes in the first couple of chapters have too many unrelated sets of people.

When there's not some major action by page 10 or so.

When characters have names that are too similar, or hard to pronounce.

Love, Mom and Karen

The Game of POV
Stick to the Rules.

Even though fiction grants you a lot of freedom, one rigid rule of writing is that the point of view (POV) has to remain consistent. Most novels feature a single voice telling the story because multiple points of view scatter focus.

When "I" is the eye

If your novel is written in the first person, you're not allowed to get into anyone else's thoughts:

I told Hal I was ready to get married, and he felt the acid churn in his stomach.

This is clearly wrong, since "I" has no way of knowing what is going on in the stomach of another character. The way to get around it is to say what "I" perceives:

I told Hal I was ready to get married, and he looked like he was going to throw up.

Three's a crowd

Third person narration means you're allowed to get into the head of every character in the book. But multiple points of view can weaken a scene by taking focus off the main character.

Marcia announced she was ready to get married, and Hal's stomach turned over. *I'm not ready for this!* he thought. Marcia smiled as excitement filled her. She couldn't wait!

Readers might have trouble deciding who to feel sorry for. Establish who your main characters are and tell most of the story through their POV:

Marcia announced she was ready to get married, and Hal's stomach turned over. *I'm not ready for this!* he thought. Smiling, Marcia took his hand. "I was thinking of a June wedding."

When "I" is not number I

Sometimes the activities of an impressive main character are presented through the eyes of a less colorful character, the way mild-mannered Nick Carraway describes the scandals of Gatsby, or Watson extols the cleverness of Sherlock Holmes. If you're writing your story this way, beware of the tendency to tell:

I was thrilled to meet Abbie because she was such a great artist. And when she started calling me and inviting me over, I couldn't believe my luck. I went to her studio to see her paintings and they were all beautiful.

Readers can't get a clear idea of Abbie's talent, because they haven't seen it. You have to bring them along:

I'd heard from several sources that while Abbie had lots of acquaintances, her inner circle was composed of just a few long-time friends. So I was flattered when she called me. As I accepted her invitation to visit, I forced myself to speak normally and not fawn over her the way I'd seen other fans do.
She offered me a glass of lemonade, then walked me through her garden, identifying each flower, knowledgeable as any botanist. We were both perspiring from the summer sun, and my lemonade was long gone by the time she finally asked if I would like to see her studio. I nodded casually, but I was thrilled; I'd been told that an invitation to her studio was almost unheard of.

It took a few seconds for my eyes to adjust, and then I saw a watercolor propped against a chair. It was the very voice of winter, with cold gray tones, and in the clouds, the first pink of a frigid dawn. A charcoal of a nude male was so accurate that I looked away, embarrassed.

"Here's what I'm working on now." She went over to her easel and pulled off the oil cloth. "Like it?"

"Oh, Abbie!" I saw three children playing in a sandbox. There were scratched knees, straggly pig tails, striped shirts, and chubby feet half-buried in sand. Plastic animals resided in pail-shaped castles. A purple horse chatted easily with a gorilla. In the distance sat the mothers, swapping gossip, drinking bottled water. "I love it!"

When your narrator is impersonal

Make sure your omniscient POV doesn't put distance between your story and your readers:

Abbie's beautiful pictures hung all over; there was a wonderful watercolor of a winter scene propped against a chair, and a charcoal of a nude male on the wall. Her best work, an oil on canvas of children playing in a sandbox, was on her easel.

Since the narrator isn't a character readers have gotten to know, judgements of "wonderful" or "accurate" or even Abbie's "best work" don't make as much of an impact - again, it's a case of readers being told what to think.

When characters talk about themselves

Check out how much less interesting Abbie's work sounds from her POV:

I was proud of the winter scene because I'd been told it actually made people shiver with gloom. The charcoal of a nude male was especially accurate because the model, a handsome boy young enough to be my son, became my lover for three weeks. But it was the playground painting that everyone loved most; they said the three little children playing in the sandbox were so charming.

Ask yourself, *Am I telling my story using the best POV?*

Right It

At the end of each chapter, readers should have more information or a deeper understanding of characters than when the chapter began.

A Blast From the Past

How the past can be discovered in the present and change the future.

Sometimes characters come upon old correspondence that opens up a mystery or answers an age-old question. Other times characters are forced to confront their own past and see how it has shaped their current behavior. Flashbacks are an effective vehicle for promoting transformation in your main character, but too often they're abrupt, clumsy, or sound contrived.

Letters and the old diary in the attic

When you write about a 21st-century housewife reading a hundred-year old diary she found in her attic, you set yourself the challenge of telling two stories.

Lure readers in and make them care about both. Be sure the voice of your "now" character is different from your "then" character.

In *I Know This Much is True* by Wally Lamb, the main character has his grandfather's memoirs transcribed from Italian to English. The Old-World arrogance of the Sicilian grandfather is the opposite of the main character's crippling insecurity. Readers get lost in both stories.

Flashbacks

A flashback can be a brief passage in italics, or a whole chapter. It can even be a whole book, with a Prologue and an Epilogue that take place in the present. Sometimes a book has multiple flashbacks, and sometimes there are flashbacks within flashbacks.

Although most of *Early From the Dance* by David Payne takes place in the past, chapter one features the main character as he is today - burnt out, cynical, drunk and belligerent. A phone call telling him about the death of someone he used to know triggers painful, powerful memories of a boyhood tragedy. Right away readers want to know why this character, a talented artist who seems to have it all, is so bitter. David Payne succeeds in making readers ask *What happened?*

Even better, readers wonder, *What happens next?*

Be clear

When you move from present to past, or past to present, it has to be immediately clear to readers. If it's a brief flashback, use italics.

>**"You're driving me crazy," Carl said. "You never shut up!"**
>**Izzy lowered her head, shamed. It was what her father used to say as he took out the belt and made her pull her pants down. *I've had it up to here with you, young lady!* "I'm sorry, Carl. I'll try to be quiet."**

For full-blown flashbacks, don't be coy. Start a new chapter or a new section, and announce the date.

Nothing is more annoying to readers than being confused. Is this happening now? Or did it happen years ago?

If your story takes place mostly in the past, then suddenly joins the characters in the present, make sure you haven't hurried the process. Like a factory worker punching out at quarter of five the Friday before a three-day weekend, some writers think that once they've told the bulk of the story, they're pretty much done.

Imagine getting caught up in twenty exciting chapters about a wild, uninhibited Bohemian 1960s summer with a woman who experiments with sex and drugs and yoga, has spiritual epiphanies, and marches in anti-war protests.

Then imagine discovering that the last chapter, which takes place thirty years later, briskly sums up her current situation like a newspaper article:

After college she fooled around for a few years, but then got a job as an accountant. Within five years she worked her way up to management, and then she started her own firm, which was very successful. She wore a suit to work every day, and people did what she told them to do. She'd been married, but got divorced when she discovered her husband was cheating on her. There'd been no men since then, and none of her kids were talking to her. She checked her watch and saw that it was time to visit her mother at the nursing home. Two years earlier, her mother had had a stroke that left her paralyzed and blind. Her father had died five years earlier, from diabetes.

You'd want so many more details - who did she marry? How long were they married? Why was he cheating on her? How many kids did they have? Why aren't they speaking to her?

Readers will remember that they hated an ending more than they'll remember they loved the beginning and the middle.

Too many flashbacks spoil the book

It's fun to delve into the history of a character. But too many flashbacks complicate, confuse, and irritate if they chronicle more than a few time periods. Don't expect readers to keep track of multiple locations and dates - it's too much work. Plus it interrupts the flow and blocks the sense of immediacy you've worked so hard to achieve.

Ask yourself, *What is the purpose of my flashback? How does it impact the present? How does it change my main characters?*

Prologue Pros and Cons

Make sure yours says "Something exciting is
going to happen!" not "I'm a writer who lacks skill."

A Prologue is usually a peek into the climax of a book; a promise the writer makes
to the reader. But don't depend on your Prologue to make up for a dull beginning.

Diagnosis: SPD

A writer goes to the doctor complaining of occasional weakness. "I start out okay, but then I lose my energy."

The doctor reviews the writer's symptoms - uneven pace, cloudy thinking, and a pronounced but undefinable sense that something just feels "wrong." Soberly, he delivers his diagnosis: Severe Prologue Dependency.

"You're relying on a strong Prologue to get you through," he said, "instead of treating the underlying problem."

"Is that fatal?" asks the writer anxiously.

"Almost never. The good news is, there is a proven cure."

"Thank God. But what's the bad news?"

"The bad news is, you can't keep writing this way."

The writers nods. "Okay, sure, whatever you say." He reaches for his Prologue.

"No," says the doctor, snatching it away.

"Come on! Just one more time. Then never again."

"Don't you get it? You have to stop *now*."

The writer watches in horror as the doctor tears up the Prologue and throws it into the trash.

"What are you doing? Give that to me! I need it!"

Pushing the doctor out of the way, the writer crouches by the wastebasket, retrieving pieces of his Prologue, trembling and trying to put it back together. But it's no use. He starts to cry. His Prologue... gone!

"You'll be fine," says the doctor, helping him to his feet. "I've seen cases much worse than this recover completely."

Why have one?

Your Prologue is an immediate grab - the scene of a crime, the celebration of a hard-earned award, the culmination of years of work. *Lucy* is Donald Johanson's non-fiction account of how he discovered a 3.4 million-year-old skeleton. Instead of beginning the book with the history of paleoanthropology, he uses a Prologue to draw readers in with a fascinating description of how he found an ancient knee joint in an Ethiopian desert.

Prologues in fiction

Stories that begin by establishing status quo are often about unremarkable circumstances, which makes it hard to engage readers right away. So some writers use a Prologue to stimulate intrigue and make readers think, *I can't wait to see what led up to this!*

Consider the following scene:

Alice came home to a house full of kids and no adults.

"Where's your father?" she asked in alarm. All those kids and no one watching them! "Johnny, who said you could have so many friends over?"

"Dad said it would be okay," Johnny said defensively.

Alice surveyed the sea of young faces, and everyone seemed okay. Maybe none of them would mention to their parents that they'd spent the afternoon unattended. Wasn't that just like Bob to say *Go ahead, invite friends over,* then skip out. Probably his brother George's idea; since being dumped by his wife of twenty years, George had done nothing but disrupt the household, showing up with beer and pot, and spending numerous nights on the couch.

"Who would like cookies?" Alice asked the kids. She didn't blame Julie for leaving. George was impossible to live with. Even Bob said so - as kids they fought all the time. Not just argued, but engaged in physical combat, and once, when Bob was eleven, he wound up in the hospital with a broken wrist.

Watch how the drama accelerates when this action-packed Prologue appears first:

From the window, Alice watched the police stuff swearing, struggling Bob into the squad car. Sirens blaring and lights flashing, and nosey neighbors on their porches, She held Johnny tight, trying to cover his eyes so that he wouldn't see his father being taken away. If only she'd said No when George asked if he could move in with them for a few days! If only she'd known it would lead to a vicious love triangle, kidnaping, and murder!

Don't depend on an artificial hook

Too many writers think that if they've delivered a blockbuster Prologue, their readers will be willing to sit through less exciting scenes. Guess what? Some won't want to!

Don't rely on your Prologue to take the place of strong, responsible writing, and don't let your action dip.

Ask yourself, *Does my Prologue serve its purpose? Have I followed through with the same intensity for the rest of my book?*

Right It

Read. Every. Word.
Out. Loud. Slowly. And.
Listen. Carefully.

Overcome Your Bad Habits
by Rebecca Leo

In *A Writer Teaches Writing*, author Donald Murray says that writing is rewriting. The revision stage, however, is the place where many become blocked. Completing the first draft is such a relief! But afterwards, some writers don't have energy left to think again about their story and how they have written it. Those who are emotionally attached to their manuscript (that includes most of us) resist making changes. Others are eager to improve their manuscript but don't know how.

From writing we learn not only about our topics and ourselves, but also about writing. Like cooking, painting and speaking a foreign language, writing improves with practice. My writing partners and I agree that our writing is always better at the end of the book than the beginning. We feel compelled to go back and revise in order to match the quality of the beginning to that achieved in the end. By the end of the next draft, we see again that our more recent writing is superior. When to stop?

The revision process requires that we become conscious of the components of effective writing in order to evaluate and refine our own work.

Revising is to See Again

Look at your topic and prose in a new way, i.e., as a reader. Observe your own responses as you read: how the writing makes you feel, what you like, what you don't, and why.

Paragraphs
Look at the shape of the text on the page and ask if it is accessible. Generally, short is more inviting than long. This pertains to paragraphs as well as chapters. Paragraphs that go on for more than half a page become a barrier to readers. Try to break your text into accessible bits.

Chapters
The chapters in *The DaVinci Code* by Dan Brown run from one to nine pages, but most are in the range of two or three. Exceptionally short for such an ambitious book, but it makes the story accessible. Readers can finish a chapter even if they only have a few minutes.

Dialogue

Books with long, dense paragraphs are scarce on dialogue. The convention of beginning a new paragraph for each change of speaker forces a writer to begin new paragraphs frequently. But when speech is reported rather than shown, an entire conversation can be recounted in a single paragraph. If you see this in your writing, consider changing some of the indirect speech to dialogue. Not only will it look more appealing; it will enable readers to hear the characters and know them better through how they talk.

Descriptions

Try to see characters, settings, and actions as the prose actually describes them. If the impact is not as you intended, experiment with new expressions, structures and images.

-ly Words

Question each word that ends in "ly." Most are adverbs that may be unnecessary. They can distract rather than add meaning. This happens when an adverb substitutes for a precise verb, as in "slowly got himself out of bed" rather than "dragged himself." Adverbs can also be redundant as in "shouted loudly into the phone" or "the diamond sparkled brightly on her finger." Be especially alert when two words ending in "ly" are used in one sentence.

Meals were invariably served punctually at the same time they had been served for forty years.

One "ly" has to go.

Revising is to Think Again

Characters

Think about characters and their motives. Are they believable? Would a person really behave, feel, think or talk that way? Have you shown enough about the characters to enable readers to relate? To feel suspicion, respect, affection, disgust, sympathy?

Readers

Do readers need to know this, that and the other thing in order to follow the story and understand the characters? If not, cast this, that and the other thing overboard.

Organization

Think about the sequence of events and ideas. Are they arranged to produce optimum impact in terms of interest, suspense, and desire to know more? Consider changes that will enhance. Chronological order is not the only way to go.

The punch

My writing partner, Tom, has written "Don't telegraph the punch" on my manuscripts more times than I care to admit. He explains, "Let the action show what happens; don't tell readers in advance."

Dad's reply surprised Jacqueline. "Well, you know what?" he said. "Your smoking is offensive to me."

When you tell readers how they're supposed to interpret something (in this case, be surprised) you dilute the impact. Let readers react to Dad's words firsthand along with Jacqueline.

Revising is to Listen Again

Read aloud

An essential part of listening again is reading aloud. Many books, both fiction and nonfiction, are now put on audiotape or CD for "readers" to hear. Make sure the sound of your prose is "ear-ready." Listen for features that can annoy or distract readers

Avoid repetition of sounds

The use of any major word (excluding articles and some prepositions) more than once in a sentence or twice in a paragraph is suspect.

> **"We're going out for a walk," he told the others, and taking my hand, he led me out. He didn't say anything until we were far out of range.**

Re-write to eliminate two of the three "out"s:

> **"We're going for a walk," he told the others, and taking my hand, he led me out. He didn't say anything until we reached the end of the driveway.**

Watch for homonyms

Avoid overuse of words that sound alike even if they have different meanings. To our ears, it's all the same. So in addition to guarding against using words such as "said" or "people" three times in a paragraph, we must be aware of words like "to," "two," "too;" "so," "sow," and "sew;" "through" and "threw," or "do," "due," and "dew."

The following paragraph has the same word sound nine times in two sentences:

> **Jeff stood like a rock in a current while pedestrians streamed by, trying to figure out what to do, too unfamiliar to even know what questions to ask. How stupid, not to listen when Terry, who came to the city all the time, tried to tell him where to go.**

A solution: The imagery in the first clause is vivid, it must be kept. But the following phrase is ambiguous and might make the reader pause to wonder whether it's Jeff or the pedestrians who are "trying to figure out what to do." Resolving that problem eliminates one of the "to"s, and several others drop away with a little tweaking, reducing the total to three:

Jeff stood like a rock in a current while pedestrians streamed by. He wondered what to do, but everything was so unfamiliar that he didn't even know what questions to ask. How stupid, not listening when Terry, who came to the city all the time, tried telling him where he should go.

Listening to your own prose will reveal irritations to the ear. Fix them.

Watch out for redundancies

Telling readers the obvious is boring, and it's a sure way to lose them. Yet we do it all the time as in "burned herself on the hot ember," "flew through the air," "ran rapidly down the hill," or "the fire burned in the potbelly stove." What else would a fire do besides burn?

Likewise, "Sally nodded her head and responded with a coy smile" is stating the obvious. Have you ever known anyone to nod with a body part other than the head?

Let the language do its work; spare your readers the unnecessary helpers.

If you show, don't tell

Telling readers what they already know insults their intelligence and wastes their time. I am one of the biggest culprits here. Over and over my writing partners say, "You don't have to tell us that because you've already shown it."

David whacked the child's hand with slaps that turned his skin crimson. Jon screamed and ran toward the back door. Halfway there, he fell face down on the grass.

"Stupid little bastard, I'll put him in his room," David told Jacqueline. Then he roughly picked the boy up and disappeared inside the house.

Jacqueline cringed at how David had hit Jonathon and dragged him screaming into the house.

The first two paragraphs show; the third tells. Paragraph three is not necessary, therefore, it's clutter.

Avoid repetitive sentence

It's monotonous and unnecessary. The English language allows for endless flexibility. Use it. To prevent a lapse in attention and escape the brand of amateur, vary the order of sentence components. Consider how dull the following account from an early draft of my novel sounds:

Magic had hired two helpers for the day to cut and haul bananas to the plant. He left early with Richard and Clayton at his side to get the job done. He asked Jacqueline to bring lunch for them.

Combining two sentences makes the passage more concise and less monotonous:

Magic had hired two helpers for the day to cut and haul bananas to the plant. He left early with Richard and Clayton, requesting that Jacqueline bring lunch for them.

Revising is to Choose Again

**Cut out
distractions**

When words or expressions sound inauthentic or when they distract readers, it's time to consider another option.

An example from my novel: **Jacqueline was fatigued.** Robin asked, "Why not simply 'tired'?"

Consider this: **Pieces of the shroud of silence that occluded any reference to sexuality in her mother's household extended all the way across the Caribbean.**

I changed it to: **She still couldn't talk about sex.**

When composing submission letters to agents I have been tempted to call my book a *bildungsroman.* Regardless of how absolutely perfect the definition of this word is for my book, I have resisted using it, knowing it could send agents to the dictionary, and they might not return to my letter.

**Don't use
excessive detail**

While specific details are usually desirable, excessive details can distract readers from the drama of the story.

David passed out just as his wife entered the kitchen. Blood dripped from his ears onto the dirty polyurethaned oak floor.

At this dramatic moment, neither character nor an observer would focus on the floor's surface. Likewise, the reader's attention should not be brought to the finish, composition, or condition of the floor.

Watch out for dust bunnies

Unconscious habits pop up in our manuscripts like dust bunnies, requiring constant vigilance. These bunnies, often invisible to us, can annoy readers - even on the subconscious level - and create a barrier between reader and story. Some of these problems get past editors and make it into published books. Others play a role in preventing a good story from ever being published. Becoming conscious of such habits is the first step toward editing them out.

Verbs In Action

Is that redundant or what?
By Rebecca Leo

Verbs are action words, but some are definitely more active than others. You can improve your writing by tracking down the weak verbs and replacing them with words that have more power, are more precise, and are shorter, as in less wordy. Key criteria are: active, specific, short, strong.

Always question the inactive verb

Locate all forms of "to be" including "is," "are," "am," "was," "were," "been," and "be" itself, as in "will be," "would be," and "should be." This does not mean eliminate all of them. Just question them. First drafts abound with these lazy, inactive and often unnecessary verbs.

Choose active

	Before	**After**
	The baby was what mattered now.	Only the baby mattered now.
	They must all be questioned.	We must question them all.
	All of them must be eliminated.	We must eliminate them all.

Those "be"s are hard to stop!

How would you fix the following?

> **"It won't be easy. But I'll be patient, no matter how long it takes. There has to be a solution."**

59

Use Specific Verbs

The English language has plenty of them. Instead of hitching a prepositional phrase or an adverb to a general verb, use a specific verb.

Which works better?

He questioned me on how long I had known D.	He asked how long I had known D.
Ted put the domino down forcefully.	Ted slammed the domino on the table.
Louis likes the painting a lot.	Louis adores the painting.
Tony died after excessive inhalation of water.	Tony drowned.

Don't dilute your action

Instead of...	Use...
walked slowly	sauntered, strolled
moved quickly	rushed, ran, hurried
hold tightly	squeeze, grasp

How can you improve these?

touch lovingly
write sloppily
look at carefully
eat quickly
move in a circle
speak emphatically
put food on a table
came into the room

Verb Phrases

Watch out for those meandering strings of verbs and modifiers. The lone active verb is stronger than a verb phrase.

Keep it short	**Before**	**After**
	The venom continued pouring out of David's mouth.	Venom spewed from David's mouth.
	I got busy unpacking while David went for cleaning supplies. He returned carrying broom, bucket, and mop	I unpacked while David went out and got a broom, bucket, and mop.
	David, sitting in the back seat, kept busy reading *The Gleaner*.	David sat in back reading *The Gleaner*.
Which sounds better?	I am aware of the cost.	I know the cost.
	They hope to visit Grandma.	They have been hoping to visit Grandma.
	They attend the same school.	They are attending the same school.
	He is afraid of policemen.	He fears policemen.

Verbs are the Energy in our Writing

But as Goldilocks showed, neither too strong nor too weak is good. The verb power must be just right for the situation.

Too strong

My writing partners told me following was overdone:

> **Her face turned red and she started trembling. "That's an awful word," she gasped with a look of accusing horror. "Nasty, dirty."**

They convinced me to change it to:

> **Her faced reddened as she scanned the note. "That's an awful word!" her voice quavered. "Nasty, dirty."**

Again, the following was overkill:

> **"That's just the problem!" he roared like a dog with its tail caught in the door. "You don't care enough about this deal to be thinking how you can make it succeed."**

It was easily fixed by removing the simile:

> **"That's just the problem!" he roared. "You don't care enough about this deal to be thinking how you can make it succeed."**

Too weak

John fell to the floor as he passed out can be made more immediate with the two simple but stronger words: **John fainted.**

The thief left the store as fast as he could is less exciting than: **The thief darted out the back door.**

Just right

Pedestrians streamed by.

A vulture hovers overhead, gliding on currents of air as it searches for casualties of the night.

Right It

Never cut corners or coast over a scene, and never accept less than your best writing.

Rules & Regulations
Like peeing in a pool, some things just aren't allowed.

We writers are used to calling the shots. It's our book, we can do whatever we want! But a skillful writer obeys certain guidelines in order to achieve maximum impact on the reader.

You're not a kid anymore

Remember writing book reports? All the rules? No sentence fragments. No swear words. Don't end a sentence with a preposition. Make sure there's a subject and a verb in every sentence.

As a grownup, you can get away with all kinds of literary indiscretions. But violating certain rules can earn you a failing grade from an agent or a publisher.

Don't use a weak lead-in

Beginning a sentence with bland words like "shortly," "after," and "soon" makes a sentence drag. Give your sentences punch with language that's active.

D-	**A+**
After making a few phone calls, Eddie left the house	Eddie made a few phone calls then left the house.
Soon Dave showed up, and he was drunk.	Dave showed up drunk.
Shortly the salesman returned with several boxes of shoes.	The salesman returned right away with several boxes of shoes.

Don't misuse "discover" and "realize"

Discovery is a profound thing. A character discovers his mother didn't die in the fire - she's still alive! To say "She discovered that there was a run in her stocking" trivializes the beauty and the wonder of "discover." It's too strong a word here, and should be replaced with a milder word, like "noticed."

Likewise, realizing indicates a shift in thinking: "He realized he'd hated her dog all along." Too many writers overuse "realize," as in, "He realized the light had turned green and other drivers were honking their horns." In this case, "The honking horns of other cars alerted him that the light had changed" is more appropriate. There's no shift in thinking - it's just time to move his car.

Don't use words and phrases that have been rendered meaningless

We all do this. We say a movie was "incredible" or a party was "awesome." These descriptions used to have more impact, but through gradual overuse they have become less precise. To me, the fact that primates learned to walk upright and use computers - *that's* incredible.

Which gives you a clearer image of Lisa?

Lisa was drop-dead gorgeous.

Or

Lisa didn't care what fashion magazines said about short and sassy - when it came down to it, men loved long hair. Every man she'd ever been with said so. They talked about her other assets, too - her crystal blue eyes, her silky skin, her long legs and flat stomach. But the hair. That's what got them. The pick up line she heard in every bar in Boston was, "Has anyone ever told you that you have gorgeous hair?"

Don't overdo the laughter

Don't have characters laugh until they cry, gasp, or choke. Telling readers how funny something is makes it seem less funny.

Mark told Lisa how the kitten interrupted his important business meeting, and she laughed so hard she had to hold her sides.

When I'm told that Lisa laughed so hard she had to hold her sides, my instinct is to doubt that it was really *that* funny. I'd rather judge for myself.

Don't mention a good book without a good reason

Don't have your characters talk about books they're reading unless it serves the purpose of showing what a character is like.

Instead of telling readers that a character in my novel *In Love With Spring* was intellectual and drawn to deep and ponderous philosophical wonderment the way college kids often are, I showed it by having her reading *Zen and the Art of Motorcycle Maintenance* for the third time. Even if readers aren't familiar with the book, the title indicates it's heady.

But a reference to this book in an inappropriate setting wouldn't ring true. A woman who works full time and has kids, a husband, and a Victorian home she's renovating is not going to be blown away by *Zen and the Art of Motorcycle Maintenance*. Ditto Hermann Hesse, Albert Camus, and James Joyce. Double ditto Kierkegaard.

Ask yourself, *Do I need to refer to this book? Or am I just showing off?*

Oh and by the way, avoid using the cliché that a character has "lost herself" in a book.

Speaking of clichés...

Everyone knows you're supposed to avoid them like the you-know-what. But there are more out there than you think, escaping detection, pretending to be good, solid writing; overused phrases that no longer affect readers.

When Lisa found out that Mark was cheating on her, she cried bitterly.

Instead of tellling readers that Lisa cried bitterly, show it. Be inventive. Make more of an impact by letting readers *see* the bitterness.

Lisa waited until she was alone and then gave in to the tears. Really let loose, sobbing and with nose running, at times crying so hard she couldn't catch her breath. How could Mark have slept with someone else?

Don't show off

Obscure literary references might make you feel smart, but you risk annoying readers who aren't familiar with what you're talking about.

Lisa shook her head, disappointed in Maggie's Alice B. Toklas demeanor.

Sure it sounds savvy. But does it conjure up an immediate response? The last thing you want is for readers to put your book down to get online and do research. Because then what happens? That's right - while they're on line, they check their e-mail. Hours pass, and your book, crafted with such care, is lying open, face down on the couch, and the cover is curling and the spine is getting creased. All because you had to be such a pretentious smarty pants.

Don't be complicated, clever, contrived or confusing

Writers who experiment with unusual techniques limit their audience because most readers don't want a book that makes them work. They're looking for a good story that moves them or inspires them, and ideally, they can remember enough of it to talk about the next day with friends.

I once knew a writer who played literary games. In one of his stories you found out at the end that the main character was you, the reader. Very *avant garde*, but everyone in the writing group gave it a big thumbs down.

Don't leave characters hanging

"You folks ready to order?" asked the waiter, smiling professionally.

"Do you have lobster?" Lisa asked.

"Of course."

"Two steaks," Mark announced. "Well done."

Too many writers think the scene is finished. But don't forget about the waiter:

"You folks ready to order?" asked the waiter, smiling professionally.

"Do you have lobster?" Lisa asked.

"Of course."

"Two steaks," Mark announced. "Well done."

"But I was in the mood for lobster," Lisa pouted. "We had steak last night."

"Steak that you ruined," he said. "Tasted like cardboard. Didn't anyone ever teach you how to cook?"

"My mother died when I was two." She couldn't keep the resentment out of her voice. How dare he! She'd never claimed to be a good cook. "Anyway, I wanted lobster."

"Maybe I'll let you have lobster next time," he said.

As the writer, it's clear in your mind that the waiter has left. But readers will assume he's still standing there, listening to them discuss her dead mother and her inability to cook. Pay attention to the mechanics of a scene, and follow through:

"You folks ready to order?" asked the waiter, smiling professionally.

"Do you have lobster?" Lisa asked.

"Of course."

"Two steaks," Mark announced. "Well done." He handed his menu to the waiter, and dismissed him with a curt nod.

Lisa watched him leave. "But I was in the mood for lobster," she pouted. "We had steak last night."

"Steak that you ruined," he said. "Tasted like cardboard. Didn't anyone ever teach you how to cook?"

"My mother died when I was two." She couldn't keep the resentment out of her voice. How dare he! She'd never claimed to be a good cook. "Anyway, I wanted lobster."

"Maybe I'll let you have lobster next time," he said.

Be clear and precise

Ever plan what you'd say if you met a genie who would grant you one wish? Genies are mischievous creatures who love to misconstrue, and if your wish was in any way ambiguous, you might get something you didn't want. What if you said you wanted all wars to stop immediately, and the genie made every person on the planet drop dead since that was the only way to make that wish come true? How much better if you had phrased the wish differently and said you wanted the whole world to live in peace!

Every sentence in your book should reflect the same caution. Subject every word to stern and careful scrutiny to make sure it conveys exactly what you want to say.

In an episode of *Friends*, Phoebe tries to tell Rachel and Monica what her new boyfriend is like. She asks them if they saw the movie *An Officer and a Gentleman.* When they say Yes, she explains that her new boyfriend is like the guy she saw that movie with. In a TV show, it's funny that she's so imprecise. In your book? Not funny.

Learn from the masters

If you're a novelist, you should learn how to write from other novelists. The best way to do this is to attend appearances by your favorite writers. Ask questions. Listen to them describe how the process works for them, and try to take home a few good ideas. When I attended a seminar with Arthur Golden, author of *Memoirs of a Geisha,* I learned more about writing in one afternoon than I learned from a dozen books.

Is Your Book Ready to Perform?

Trim and tone your book
from start to finish to make it a winner.

These days books face stiff competition. Television, e-mail, computer games, and the phone all vie for attention. It might take years to write a book, but only a minute for someone to pick it up, flip through a few pages, and put it down to do something more interesting.

Your first
sentence has to
be a star performer

Some first sentences are well-crafted but don't offer enough intrigue:

Gloomy clouds the color of granite made everything dim and sad, without a trace of cheer anywhere.

Other first sentences jump in without grace and appeal to a reader's emotions:

Putting our dog to sleep made everyone miserable.

Your first sentence should reflect your skills as a writer at the same time that it snags the interest of readers:

On the day we put Rufus to sleep, gloomy, granite-colored clouds cast a sadness over our last walk out to the car with him.

For a first sentence that hits the ground running, use language that conveys one or more of the following: action; a sense of location, attitude, or emotion; or a strong visual lead-in.

Julia kissed Ronald and told him how happy she was for him, but instead of joining in the celebration afterwards, she sneaked out of the church and headed for the beach, not caring that the skirt of her mint green bridesmaid gown was going to get ruined, and so were those stupid mint green shoes.

A good first sentence makes readers wonder what will happen next. Review yours. What questions does it raise?

Ask yourself, *Is this the absolute best writing I'm capable of?*

Exercise strong writing

Always try to evoke an image or an emotion.

Elizabeth's bus pulled up. A young, eager Marine ahead of her started to board, then stepped back to let passengers get off. First to appear was another Marine. He was missing most of an arm, and there was a cast on one leg. Leaning heavily on crutches, he made his way down the steps. His expression was rugged, weary, wise. The Marine who was headed to war reached up to help. Their eyes met; one saw the future, one was looking at his past. Elizabeth's heart ached. She didn't know who she was more afraid for.

Make it impossible for readers to feel nothing.

Build strong characters

Force characters to make difficult decisions that will impact the rest of their lives. Donald Maas, a New York agent, advises writers to ask what's at stake for each character. The higher the stakes, the higher the tension level.

Tension is achieved when readers want to know what happens to your characters. A talented writer can coax empathy for even the most despicable character. The obvious example is Mario Puzo's *Godfather*. The man kills people! And yet, we share in his triumphs and mourn all his losses, because we get to see the tender, human side of him. That's powerful writing.

Lately there has been a trend in literature about single women who are:

Recovering from a break up
Looking for a new man
Writing articles for a fancy New York magazine
Working out mother/daughter issues
Poor, and when they open their refrigerator, all they see is moldy food or bottles of beer.

Avoid creating formula characters. Don't undermine your female characters by having them obsess about their weight or their past or future boyfriends.

Ask yourself, *Is this an authentic setting, or is it just sort of comical?* If it's "just sort of comical" ask yourself if that's good enough.

Startle readers by having your meanest character perform a good deed; or have your hero do something illegal.

Give characters depth by showing their different dimensions. Put them into difficult, challenging situations so they can discover who they are.

Make sure your characters don't sound alike. When they use the same vocabulary and have the same emotions, they're hard to tell apart. And when characters fail to distinguish themselves, they're not memorable:

"He totally annoys me," PJ said as she applied neon pink nail polish.

"Me too. So does Niles. That's, like, such a stupid name," Heather said.

"Not as stupid as Brett. It sounds like brat," Karla giggled. "Brat Connelly. That is like, so stupid. And his brother's name is Chip. Chip Connelly. Sounds like ice cream."

If more than two characters sound the same, see if anyone is expendable. Unnecessary characters dilute impact.

Put in the time

A lazy writer tells how a character feels:

Bonnie was seeing several men at the same time, even though it made her feel guilty.

A skillful writer takes the time to show:

Bonnie sat in front of the mirror and looked at her watch - twenty minutes before Eugene would arrive. Twenty minutes to wash off Brad's kisses. Her hair smelled like his cologne. What if Eugene recognized it as a man's scent? What if he asked her if she'd been with someone else? With an uneasy laugh, she thought about coming clean with him; with them all. God, what a relief that would be! Leaning forward, she inspected her eye shadow, touched up her blush, refreshed her mascara, then spritzed jasmine fragrance on her neck.

Include team players

Make sure your incidental characters serve a purpose. Watch how a friendly waitress can show how rude your character is to the working class.

When she walked up, she was all smiles. Cute in her red and white checkered apron.
   "Take your order?" she greeted us.
   I told her I'd have the fried chicken. She nodded and wrote it down on her little pad. Then she looked at Graham. I saw he was frowning.

"This is the whole menu?" he asked.

"It's written on both sides."

He turned it over, barely glanced at the back, then sighed like it was the end of the world. "Everything here is so greasy. Makes you wonder how many people eat here and die young."

Her smile faded as she waited for him to decide. He took his time, flipping the menu over, back and forth, as if every single item was dog shit. Finally he just handed it to her.

"Coffee. Black," he said.

An exchange with a snobby salesperson allows readers to see how timid your main character is.

I looked at the dresses, but they were too expensive, or wouldn't have looked good on me. An unsmiling saleswoman wearing a lot of makeup came over.

"Help you?" she asked in a chilly, uninterested tone.

"No, thank you. I'm just looking."

"Well what are you looking *for*. This is the junior section."

I looked at the dress I had pulled out. She was right. It was too tight, too young, too short, too low cut. How embarrassing! I felt like I was a hundred years old.

"We have a rack of markdowns, if you're interested." She pointed toward the back of the store. "Maybe you could find something there."

"Actually, I'm running late. I have to go. Thanks for your help!" I hurried out.

Not everyone finishes the race

I lost someone very dear to me. I loved her, but one day she had to leave, and I knew I would never see her again.

Her name was Linnie, and she was a character in my novel *Blue or Blue Skies*. Like me, she was a struggling writer. At the end of the book I set her on the road to publication after years of heartbreak, faith, and hard work. What a blast, to watch her succeed! Then one day my writing partner Rebecca challenged me to justify Linnie's part in the book.

"She's the... she always... she's the narrator's best friend!" I sputtered.

"But she doesn't serve a purpose," Rebecca said.

I sat back with the beginning of a headache. I'd been working on *Blue or Blue Skies* for almost fifteen years. Linnie had been there since the beginning. In my head, she was so much a part of the story. But Rebecca was right. Technically, Linnie added nothing. And as my other partner Tom said, "Whatever doesn't add *takes away.*"

Make sure every character has a definite role to play.

Don't ease up in the home stretch

Almost done, and now you can relax! All you have to do is tie up a few loose ends. This part's easy. Right?

Wrong. Readers can tell when a writer has reached what I call the "point of disengagement;" when it's no longer about writing - it's about finishing.

The ending is one of the three most important parts of the book (the other two are the beginning and the middle!) You're tired. But you have to keep going; in fact, you need an extra burst of energy here, to create an ending that will satisfy readers.

The best novels are about transformation. In the end your main characters should be different from how they were when the book began. They should endure suffering, make tough decisions, and confront the rest of their life with new hard-earned wisdom.

Ask yourself, *What did each character lose? What did each gain?*

Join or Start a Writers Group
The best way to improve your writing is to work with other writers.

Just so you know, I don't always get to be the bully. I've been on the unhappy receiving end of harsh criticism many times - with my writing group, and for three months when I hired a writing coach. Feedback is crucial to the revision process.

Experts agree

Living near Boston means getting to see the best writers on the planet when they come to town. I love when they read from their latest book and talk about how they got the idea. Usually people in the audience are writers too, and during the question and answer period, someone always asks, *What advice can you give other writers?* The answer never varies: *Be in a writers group.*

Stick with your own kind

It's been my experience that the best groups are made up of writers who are alike - all novelists, all poets, or all short story authors. Each genre presents a different set of dynamics. Poems and short stories can be read and critiqued in a single sitting, but novels require that chapters be taken home, and each member of the group has to remember what happened in the chapter before. Some writers only like novels and get impatient with shorter fiction. Others prefer stories and poems because they don't have time to read entire manuscripts.

Limit the number of members so you can spend plenty of time with each other's work. My group has only three members, but our meetings often last five hours.

Be serious

If you start a group by putting an ad in the local newspaper or posting a notice at libraries, book-stores, and coffee shops, make it clear that only serious writers need apply.

If you're planning to join an existing group, make sure the other members are committed to working together.

Be tough

Weed out the writers who aren't ready to be in a serious group by enforcing inflexible rules: No canceling without a good reason. No showing up without material. No saying you couldn't read someone else's chapter because you were too busy. Allow for some exceptions, but act sullen and make them miserable if they try it again.

Take advantage of your writing partners

They are there to help you. Use them. Their feedback is the knowledge you need to write a better book.

Ask what they liked; what they thought worked well, made them think, created suspense, made them want to read more.

Ask what they didn't like, and listen carefully when they explain.

When bad news is good news

Criticism is more helpful than praise. Criticism that's logical, precise, and followed by advice about how to fix something is best.

One night my partner Tom ripped into the main character of my novel *On Air*, saying he was unsubstantial, unconvincing, and not interesting. He said I could do better, I had to dig deeper. He told me I hadn't developed the character at all. I cried the whole way home. Advice stings when it hits a nerve.

The next day (when I could bear to look at my manuscript again) I started over, right from the very first sentence, determined to dig deeper. Right away new facets of my character's personality emerged, giving him more dimension.

It works both ways

Critiquing the work of others helps your writing. Being forced to clarify what's wrong with someone else's writing helps you spot flaws in your own.

But don't just say you hate something. Have a reason: It was clumsy. Felt contrived. Didn't move you. Didn't belong.

A word to the "Why?"s

Writers can be stubborn, defensive creatures who want to know *why* they have to change something. It makes sense to them. It sounds good! Why should they change it?

My rule is: if one writing partner questions something, I examine it with an open mind. If both partners question the same thing for the same reason, I change it. Why waste everyone's time trying to defend what I've written? I'm not going to be there to explain my reasoning to every single reader. Almost always, the change is an improvement.

Right It

Get feedback, especially from other writers. Be more interested in fixing problems than in being defensive.

Sample Page
Before feedback and after

So many writers come to me thinking they're done with a chapter or scene, but as I review it, I see plenty of opportunities for improvement. The following needs technical and stylistic editing:

Before

I was about to go a meeting before I was stopped by my co-worker, Colleen, who seemed sort of desperate.

"What's wrong?" I demanded.

"Oh!" she cried, reaching for a Kleenex. "I think I'm going to be fired!" She shouted hysterically.

"What makes you think that?" I asked, patting her back. "Has something happened?"

"Well," she sobbed. "If you count sleeping with your boss as "something." Then yes."

My mouth fell open and my eyes grew wide. Colleen was sleeping with the boss? Anger filled me. I was sleeping with the boss too.

Feedback

"I was about to go to the meeting" is weak. Take out "seemed" and "sort of." They don't add anything.

"Demanded" is too strong here.

Don't use product names like Kleenex, Xerox, BandAid, or Styrofoam without the trademark symbol.

Never use more than one attribute (cried, shouted) in a single paragraph. To say she "shouted" is hard to visualize; aren't they at work? Would she really cry and shout? And to say the shouting is hysterical is way overdone.

"Did something happen?" is more authentic than "Has something happened?"

To say she's sobbing is heavy handed - you're going way overboard with this.

Mouths falling open and eyes growing wide are clichés.

After

I was on my way to a meeting when my co-worker Colleen stopped me in the hall. She looked desperate.

"What's wrong?" I asked.

"Oh God." She dug in her purse for a tissue, found one, and blew her nose. "I think I'm going to be fired!"

"What? Why? Did something happen?"

"Well," she said, "if you count sleeping with your boss as 'something' then Yes."

I took a step back, didn't know what to say. What *could* I say? I was sleeping with the boss too.

Review

You've reached the end of my book, but maybe not the end of yours.

Hey, you think it's fun to tell you your book isn't ready? You think I like seeing the look on your face when I say you have to go over it again? I know you're sick of it! But remember how you felt when you first decided to write a book? Maybe it came to you in a sudden blast; maybe it took months of growing excitement. You sat down and started to write, and you had big plans. You weren't going to write a mediocre book, you were going to write a *great book*. And nothing becomes great without time and hard work.

Admit that your book isn't perfect yet

Don't send your book out if you know in your gut that some parts aren't as good as they could be. Too many writers think agents or publishers will overlook sloppy work if the story is good.

Picture yourself handing your book to the person you admire most, and having to sit there while they read the whole thing out loud. How would you feel? Confident? Nervous? Embarrassed?

Your first sentence

Your first sentence has to be memorable. What questions does it raise? What emotions?

Since your first sentence can form your reader's first impression, do the best writing of your life. Then write the rest of the book with the same care.

Read every word out loud

Read slowly and pay attention! If your mind wanders, concentrate harder, or take a break. Don't rush this process, and don't skip it. When clients show me their revised chapters, I can always tell which parts they read out loud and which parts they didn't.

Eliminate empty words and phrases

Avoid using non-specific words that don't conjure up an image or evoke an emotion. Be on the lookout for sentence-weakening words like "somewhat," "rather," "quite." Don't overuse "very" and "really."

Use strong language

Replace cumbersome phrases with more precise single words. Watch for -ly words, and avoid using an adverb to describe an action if a single word can handle the job. Instead of "played loudly," say "blared."

Go from static to dynamic

Give a scene more impact by letting readers experience it firsthand through dialogue. Avoid using language that sounds contrived, and make sure that every line of dialogue relays information, develops a character, or moves the story forward. Don't miss opportunities to show instead of tell. Be clear and direct.

Every scene should accomplish something. At the end of each chapter, readers should know something new.

Spend time with your characters

Great novels have great characters. Are yours genuine? Likeable? Memorable? What's at stake for each main character? Does everyone have a distinctive voice and a role to play? Review the transformation of your characters. What was lost? What was gained?

All the facts, Ma'am

Do your readers have all the facts? Don't presume. Double-check everything. Keep track of what you know, what readers know, and what characters know. During the revision process, shuffling scenes can cause characters to act out of a knowledge they haven't acquired yet. Guess who picks up on stuff like that? Publishers and agents. They're quick to spot sloppy writing and aren't going to give you a second chance.

Make sure the ending works as hard as you did

How will readers feel when they get to the last sentence in your book? Will they be moved? Lost in thought? Will they tell a co-worker or friend about your book?

The highest praise from a reader is *I didn't want the book to end!* Constantly strive for that.

Get feedback

The best way to find out if your book really is as good as you think is to get feedback from other writers. Be open to advice. Don't be defensive. Criticism is more helpful than praise. Praise is nice, but it doesn't lead to transformation. Be willing to try a new way. You have nothing to lose, and you might be surprised that it sounds better.

Fix it!

The following scene has real problems, but now you know how to recognize what's wrong and why.

I went to the grocery store and picked up groceries and drove home. The light on the answering machine was blinking and I pressed the message button and heard the voice of Sam, my fiance.

"Jeannette!" he yelped. "I need you to meet me at the Burger King on Route 1! It's important!" he concluded on a anxious note.

That was the only message on the machine. As my stomach started churning anxiously, I thought to myself, What could he want? What was wrong? What was going on? I wondered why he had called and left such an urgent message.

I put all the groceries away and when I went to the Burger King he was there. I went over and he kissed me. Soon he told me that he had met someone else and she was carrying his child. All the way home I cried as if my heart would break in two.

There are two ways to tell a story

You can report a series of events featuring boring characters without clear motives in difficult-to-picture situations. Or you can use authentic-sounding dialogue to craft scenes, letting the story unfold, engaging readers, and earning their sympathy for characters who are unforgettable as they react to challenging circumstances.

Which way will you do it?

The best advice

Don't rush the revision process. Don't consider your book done if you know it's not. Be brutal. If you can point to even one scene that doesn't evoke an emotion, move the story forward, or develop characters, then it's not ready. Too many writers get bored or impatient, and lose focus. When I suggest they revise something, they say wearily, "Oh, I'm so sick of doing that part. I'm sure it's okay."

Ask yourself, *Is it my dream to write a book that's just "okay?"*